Sailing the Stars

by Anne Cambal

Editorial Offices: Glenview, Illinois • Parsippany, New Jersey • New York, New York
Sales Offices: Needham, Massachusetts • Duluth, Georgia • Glenview, Illinois
Coppell, Texas • Ontario, California • Mesa, Arizona

ISBN: 0-328-13569-0

11 12 13 14 15 16 V054 16 15 14 13 12 11 10

CONTENTS

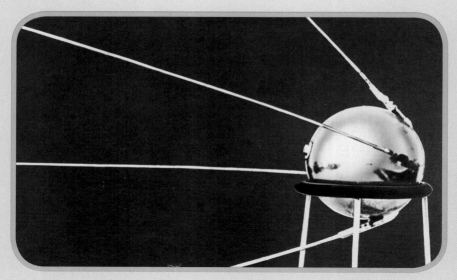

Sputnik I was the first satellite to be launched into space.

Chapter 1: Pioneers in Space

People have dreamed of space travel for many years, but it wasn't until the late 1950s that these dreams began to come true.

After World War II, the United States and the Union of Soviet Socialist Republics (USSR) were enemies in the Cold War. Instead of fighting each other face to face, the two nations tried to increase their influence all over the world. Each country wanted to be the first in space, in part to prove that its own society was the best.

The USSR struck first. On October 4, 1957, the USSR sent the first manufactured satellite, *Sputnik I*, into space. A satellite is something that orbits, or travels around, a larger body in space. For example, the moon is a satellite of Earth.

One month later, the USSR launched *Sputnik II*. It carried the first live animal in space, a dog named Laika.

The United States hurried to catch up. Almost three months after the launch of *Sputnik II*, the United States launched *Explorer I*. Through this mission, scientists learned that Earth is surrounded by magnetic radiation belts.

On October 1, 1958, the National Aeronautics and Space Administration (NASA) was created. NASA researches, plans, constructs, and manages the U.S. space program.

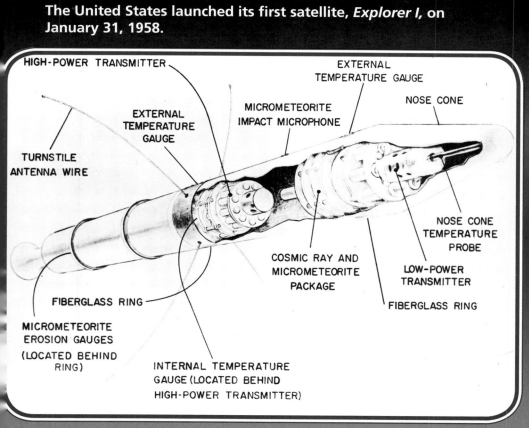

The United States launched its first satellite, *Explorer I*, on January 31, 1958.

HIGH-POWER TRANSMITTER

EXTERNAL TEMPERATURE GAUGE

NOSE CONE

EXTERNAL TEMPERATURE GAUGE

MICROMETEORITE IMPACT MICROPHONE

TURNSTILE ANTENNA WIRE

NOSE CONE TEMPERATURE PROBE

COSMIC RAY AND MICROMETEORITE PACKAGE

LOW-POWER TRANSMITTER

FIBERGLASS RING

FIBERGLASS RING

MICROMETEORITE EROSION GAUGES (LOCATED BEHIND RING)

INTERNAL TEMPERATURE GAUGE (LOCATED BEHIND HIGH-POWER TRANSMITTER)

Cosmonaut Yuri Gagarin, 1961

Astronaut John Glenn, 1961

Astronaut Alan B. Shepard, Jr., 1961

What's in a Name?

astronaut: a person who travels beyond Earth's atmosphere; a trainee for space flight. This term is also used specifically to describe such a person in the U.S. space program, as opposed to other space programs.

cosmonaut: an astronaut of the USSR—now the Russian—space program

spationaut: an astronaut of France

taikonaut or **yuhangyuan:** an astronaut of China

The United States and the USSR both wanted to be the first to put a man in space. Russian cosmonaut Yuri Gagarin won the title for the USSR. On April 12, 1961, he made one orbit around Earth in *Vostok I.*

The United States had its turn on May 5. Astronaut Alan B. Shepard, Jr., flew in space for about fifteen minutes in the *Mercury* capsule. During his flight, Shepard and his spacecraft escaped Earth's **gravity.** For about five minutes, he was weightless in space. Although his trip was short, Shepard proved that an astronaut could survive and work in space.

Unlike Gagarin, Shepard did not orbit Earth. His flight was also different in another way: The *Vostok* mission was conducted in secret. The world did not learn of the flight until after its successful completion. But 45 million Americans watched the *Mercury* mission live on television.

On February 20, 1962, John Glenn became the first American to orbit Earth. His flight lasted less than five hours, in which he orbited Earth three times.

When he returned, Glenn was hailed as a hero—in Washington, D.C., 250,000 people stood in the rain to cheer him. It was an exciting time in U.S. history.

Edward White was the first American to walk in space.
He holds the fueled "zip gun" in his right hand.

The 1960s saw many advances in space exploration. The first space walk was on March 18, 1965, during the USSR's *Voshkod II* mission. Co-pilot Alexei Leonov "walked" in space for about twelve minutes. His spacesuit had swelled a bit, however. He couldn't re-enter his ship until he let a little air out of the suit.

Edward White was the first American to walk in space during the *Gemini IV* mission. He used a three-jet "zip gun" to help him move around during the twenty-two-minute walk. On February 3, 1966, the USSR's *Luna IX* was the first spacecraft to land safely on the moon and send information back to Earth.

One of the greatest **accomplishments** in space travel took place on July 20, 1969. That's when the American astronaut Neil Armstrong became the first person ever to set foot on the moon. This *Apollo 11* mission also included astronauts Edwin "Buzz" Aldrin, Jr., and Michael Collins.

Armstrong and Aldrin landed on the moon's surface in the lunar module, or ship, while Collins stayed behind to operate the command module in orbit around the moon.

The landing was one of the most-watched events in the history of the world. Armstrong's first step on the lunar surface was seen by about 1 billion people! When Armstrong stepped on the surface, he said, "That's one small step for [a] man; one giant leap for mankind."

This is one of the first footprints made on the moon.

Astronaut "Buzz" Aldrin looks back at the lunar module. To the left of the module is the American flag that was planted by Armstrong and Aldrin.

There weren't any women among the original astronauts (seated) selected by NASA in 1959, nor in the second group of astronauts (standing) selected in 1962.

Chapter 2: Women in Space

The word *astronaut* comes from the Greek and Latin words for *star* and *mariner,* or *sailor.* At first, the **role** of an astronaut was seen as a pilot in space.

Early spacecraft were often modeled after military planes, and all the early astronauts were military pilots. These pilots were believed to be among the very best, especially in dangerous flying situations. The U.S. Air Force chose the first astronaut trainees. Only military pilots could qualify, and all of the candidates had to be men.

In the 1950s and 1960s, space flight was just one of many fields that were not open to American women. Women often were barred from getting the same kinds of education and experience that men could get.

Many types of careers were thought to be wrong for women. They were not expected to hold jobs that did not require motherly caring for others. Women at that time were expected to hold "women's" jobs, such as a teacher or a nurse, or low-paying jobs, such as a waitress or a maid.

Being an astronaut seemed definitely out of the question. Women were not allowed to attend pilot training in the U.S. military schools. Yet, while there were no women test pilots, things were beginning to change.

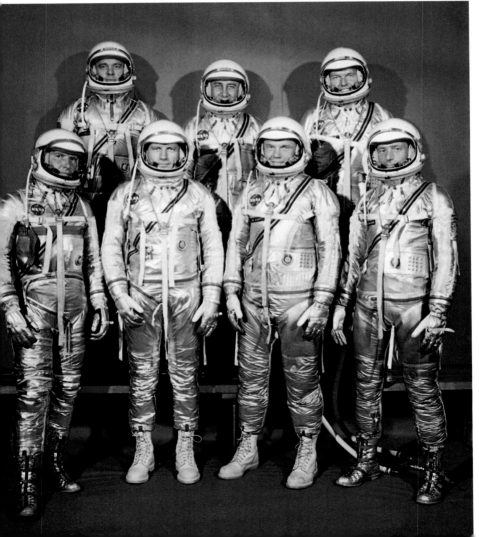

The *Columbia* space shuttle was commanded by Eileen Collins on the July 23–27, 1999, mission.

However, since the 1970s, beliefs about the proper roles for American women have changed a lot. There are women doctors, lawyers, and bankers. There are women police officers, carpenters, and truck drivers. And there are women astronauts.

In 1983, aboard the NASA space shuttle *Challenger*, Dr. Sally Ride became the first American woman to travel into space. (The first woman in space was Valentina Tereshkova on the USSR *Vostok 6* mission—twenty years before!) In 1995, Eileen M. Collins became the first woman to pilot a space shuttle. Then, in 1999, Collins set another record as the first female space shuttle commander.

Dr. Sally Ride

Dr. Sally Ride began her astronaut training in 1978. The training included parachuting, gravity, and weightlessness training, water survival, radio communications, and navigation. During training, she served as one of the support crew for space shuttle flights. As a mission specialist she also was a member of mission control.

Dr. Ride has several degrees in physics and English. She is a physicist and a college professor. Her advice to anyone interested in becoming an astronaut is to make math and science his or her **focus** of study, including physics, astronomy, and chemistry.

Dr. Mae Jemison

In 1992 Dr. Mae Jemison became the first African American woman in space, aboard the shuttle *Endeavor*. Like Sally Ride, she was a mission specialist.

When she was just 16, she was awarded a scholarship to Stanford University. Like many astronauts, Dr. Jemison studied science, including chemical engineering and physics. Then she went on to medical school and became a doctor. Dr. Jemison's careers include physician, scientist, chemical engineer, astronaut, and college professor!

Today's astronauts come from a wider variety of backgrounds. Not all astronauts are pilots, and a military background is no longer required.

Chapter 3: Space Training

Here's what it takes to apply to be a NASA astronaut:
- You must be a U.S. citizen.
- To become a pilot, you must be between 5'4" and 6'4" tall. To become a mission specialist, you must be between 4'10½" and 6'4" tall.
- You must be in good health, and your eyesight must be good.
- You must have a college degree. Candidates should have a degree in engineering, biological science, physical science, or mathematics.

Every two years, NASA reviews thousands of applications for astronaut training. From these thousands, only about one hundred men and women are chosen for interviews.

These one hundred or so people are invited to the Johnson Space Center in Houston, Texas. After they are interviewed and receive medical exams, only about twenty will be accepted.

Making the final cut does not mean that you will be an astronaut. The new trainee, or astronaut candidate, still must pass the astronaut training and evaluation course given at several NASA centers. The training and evaluation will develop the **specific** skills needed for future space missions.

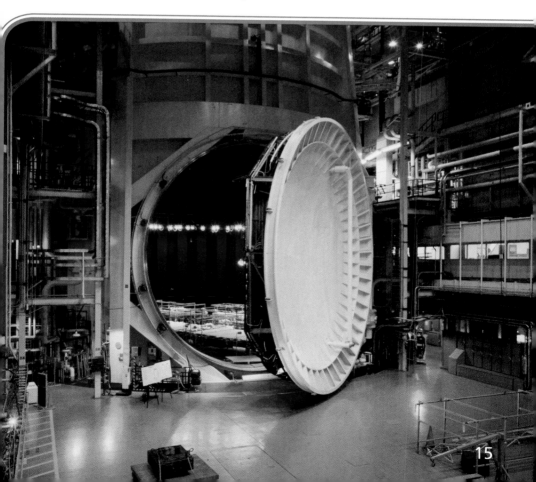

Astronaut Guion S. Bluford and Aviation Safety Officer Charles F. Hayes, on a zero-gravity training flight, are in a KC-135 aircraft, also known as the "vomit comet." It creates 30-second periods of weightlessness.

Mission Specialist Ellen Ochoa practices an emergency escape from a space shuttle at the Johnson Space Center's Mockup and Integration Laboratory (MAIL).

These women scientists are scuba diving in the Neutral Buoyancy Simulator at the Marshall Space Flight Center in Huntsville, Alabama.

Training and evaluation lasts from one to two years. Astronaut candidates must learn to live, work, handle an emergency, and survive in space.

Training includes a lot of class work and study. Trainees take many classes in science, and they also get basic medical training. They study spacecraft systems and how to do everyday things while weightless. They spend many hours flying in training aircraft and working with ground control crews. They also get a lot of practice in simulators that are like the ships or space stations they will operate. They must learn to use **monitors** and other information technology to manage conditions on their spacecraft.

Early in their training, astronaut candidates must pass a swimming test. They have to do it while wearing a flight suit and tennis shoes! This test is part of their intense emergency training. Astronauts must be ready to land in water or on land. A trainee must also learn to escape the space vehicle, whether on land or sea or by parachute while in the air. They also receive survival training in case they land in an isolated area.

Trainees also learn what it's like to work in the zero gravity of space. They do this through scuba diving and by flying in special aircraft that can create brief periods of zero gravity. You probably think that weightless flying is nothing but fun. However, weightlessness can make you feel queasy and sick. Your body must get used to it.

Dressing for Space

There is no air to breathe in space, and temperatures are extreme. To survive, an astronaut must wear a spacesuit.

In the past, each astronaut had his own spacesuit designed especially for him. Today, spacesuits are made up of separate parts. Each part of the suit locks into another part. That way, each astronaut can use different parts according to his or her own body size. Now NASA can outfit all its male and female astronauts without having to make an individual suit for each one. As you can imagine, it takes some time to suit up. Some astronauts need several hours!

The spacesuit supplies air and contains compartments for food and water. Suits are airtight, so the air inside can't leak out. They also have many layers of material to protect the astronaut from radiation, heat, cold, and flying particles in space. A spacesuit can keep an astronaut alive for up to eight hours.

The helmet is large enough for the astronaut's head to move around inside. A food bar and water bag are attached in a way that the astronaut can eat and drink inside the helmet without using his or her hands. A headphone and a microphone let the astronaut stay in touch with the onboard crew.

Spacesuits are white because white reflects heat. This helps to keep the astronaut safe—the temperature in space from direct sunlight can be more than 275° Fahrenheit!

The crew of the STS-61, the space shuttle mission to repair the *Hubble* Space Telescope

An astronaut candidate who completes the training program is not always chosen to be an astronaut. Sometimes, NASA may not have a mission for which that person's education and training are needed.

Even if a person is not selected for a mission, he or she may still be a part of NASA. Military people who have completed their training are assigned to NASA for all or part of their military careers. Civilian trainees are usually offered jobs at NASA. When NASA needs new astronauts, it is likely to choose first from its own staff.

Chapter 4: A Growing Space Family

Our study and knowledge of space has come a long way since the 1950s. We now have the *Hubble* Space Telescope and unmanned probes that show us never-before-seen pictures of our universe. Today, the space program is open to anyone who can make the grade. Instead of competing, now countries are working together to explore space.

In the beginning days of space travel, the United States and the USSR were the only countries powerful or rich enough to pursue space programs. This is why all of the space travelers in the first fifteen years were from these two countries.

Jet Propulsion Laboratory geologists Harrison Schmitt and Andrea Mosie study vesicles on a volcanic rock recovered from a lunar mission.

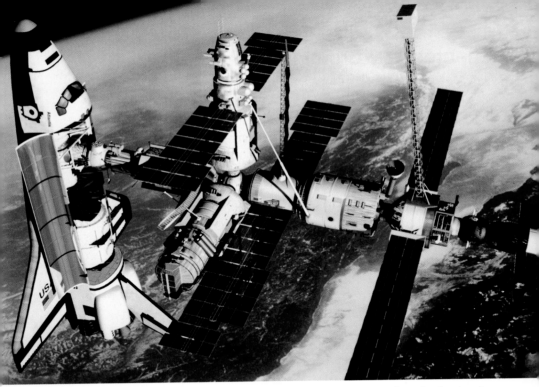

This technical image shows the Space Shuttle *Atlantis* docked to the *Kristall* module of the Russian *MIR* Space Station. The joint U.S.-Russian mission was completed in June 1995. This combination was the largest space platform ever put together in orbit.

Then, about thirty years ago, the USSR started hiring a few cosmonauts from other countries. Likewise, the United States teamed with Europeans on the *Spacelab* missions of the 1980s.

Other nations also wanted to develop their own space programs. In 1983, Canada was the first newcomer to have its own astronaut candidates. France chose its first candidates in 1985. Japan, the former West Germany, and Italy announced their own groups in the late 1980s.

The European Space Agency (ESA) was formed in 1973 but has roots as far back as the 1950s. Its member nations are the major European countries.

On Space Shuttle mission STS-9, crewmembers gather around a television screen in the *Spacelab* module. This reusable laboratory allowed scientists to perform experiments in low gravity while orbiting Earth.

They work together to share knowledge and the costs of space exploration. Many of the Canadians and Europeans who participate in our space shuttle program come from the ESA.

In 2003, China joined an exclusive club when thirty-eight-year-old former fighter pilot Yang Liwei orbited Earth fourteen times. China is now only the third country in history to have launched a person into space.

Space exploration is now a worldwide effort. Together, we can learn new and exciting things. And, if you really try, perhaps *you* will be one of the people who sail the stars!

Glossary

accomplishments *n.* successes; skills.

focus *n.* the central point of attention.

gravity *n.* the force that pulls things toward Earth's center.

monitors *n.* viewing screens that display computer input and output.

role *n.* a purpose or use for someone or something.

specific *adj.* exact; definite.